The Corps and Vietnam Remembered

(United States Marine Corps Memories of Frank James Michael Costanza)

Author: Frank James Michael Costanza

Cover Design and Illustrations: Frank James Michael Costanza

Proofreading: Joan Appleton Costanza

ISBN: 978-0-692-19513-0
Text Copyright © Frank James Michael Costanza 2018
Tables Copyright © Frank James Michael Costanza 2018
Photos Copyright © Frank James Michael Costanza 2018

All rights reserved. No part of this book may be used or reproduced in any manner whatsoever, including Internet usage, without written permission from the author. Publications are exempt in the case of brief quotations in critical reviews or articles.

Dedication

This book is dedicated to all my comrades-in-arms who served in the Vietnam War. It is also dedicated to my friends and family who have stood beside me and helped me through many trials in life resulting from my exposure to war as a impressionable youth. Finally, it is dedicated to all military veterans who suffer disabilities (visible and hidden) as a result of their combat experiences.

Preface

The Corps and Vietnam Remembered documents the memories of Marine Frank James Michael Costanza's four years of service in the United States Marine Corps. The book discusses his decision to join the Marines, basic training, Navy schools, two tours in Vietnam, and his decision to muster out. It closes with his difficult reentry into civilian life.

Introduction

The Corps and Vietnam Remembered documents the memories of Marine Frank James Michael Costanza's four years of service in the United States Marine Corps. The book discusses his decision to join the Marines, basic training, Navy schools, two tours in Vietnam, and his decision to muster out. The book closes with his difficult reentry into civilian life and somewhat tumultuous entry into the University of Maryland as an undergraduate Electrical Engineering student. It has some very graphic observations on war's effects on young servicemen.

Frank started compiling this book from notes and observations he had written over the years after his youngest son, Anthony (Tony), questioned him on Father's Day 2008 about his time served in Vietnam. Since his dad didn't talk much of his time in Vietnam, Tony wondered if he had any disturbing stories about Vietnam. Half way through Frank's response, Tony stopped his father and said what he was relaying was very hard to listen to.

The 2008 conversation served as the impetus for Frank to gather his notes and memories and put them to paper, which resulted in an unpublished book for his family, friends, and children to read as a glimpse into his formative young adult years.

The unpublished book has stirred many interesting conversations over the years and has helped Frank deal with many issues that he kept hidden within for decades. The process of putting strings of internal thoughts and emotions to paper has been very cathartic. Several readers have encouraged him to publish it more formally. The book you have before you is a product of that encouragement.

January 22, 1964: Graduation Day - MCRD San Diego

**July 25, 2014: VMFA-542 Reunion - Vietnam Memorial
49 years after landing in DaNang, walking among the departed**

The Corps and Vietnam Remembered

1963 I join the United States Marine Corps right out of High School. I had been accepted into Seminary but decided to test my vocation with a stint in the Corps. A battery of tests at Camp Smedley D. Butler in Hawaii qualifies me for Aviation Guarantee. I am going to learn Avionics and work on fighter aircraft. Of course, that means four years instead of three but I'll get a great education in Navy Schools. I get sworn into the United States Marine Corps in Hawaii on October 31. Larry Kalama (the pineapple as he likes to be called), Doug Saunders and I fly to San Francisco, California for our bus trip to Boot Camp at Marine Corps Recruit Depot (MCRD) San Diego, California.

November 3: Painted outside the receiving barracks were four lines of yellow footprints spaced exactly right for formation - our first lesson. I step into a pair of yellow footprints at MCRD San Diego and my life changes immediately and forever. I am no longer Frankie or Frank just "the lowest form of life on Earth, a boot Marine, not even able to call myself Marine yet" The Gunnery (Gunny) Sargent in charge of the Receiving Barracks and my  new Drill Instructor (DI) Sargent Warren stop in front of me and question me about my VIP status on the paperwork in front of them. Someone had put a note in my folder stating that my father was a retired "Mustang" (a Marine who started as a private then made it into the officer grades). The NCOs assumed I thought I was special because of that. Thus began a shouting match between them with me in the middle. The Gunny ordered me to smile when he said smile and to cry when he said cry. Of course, not to be outdone the Sargent gave me the same order. So, one yelled "SMILE" in one ear while the other yelled "CRY" in the other. Do you know how difficult it is to contort your face so that one side looks like it is smiling while the other side cries? This went on for several minutes until my face muscles were sore from flexing. As we are being checked in we are weighed, measured (height, chest size, etc.) and looked over physically every way possible. I am told my height was 5' 1½". My DI states that you need to be 5' 2" to be a Marine Recruit so he orders me to report at 0600 the next day to be re-measured. The next morning, I am told that I am 5' 1⅞" and my DI says the he will "GIVE: me the ⅛" because he wants his VIP in his platoon. I am in for some deep shit for the next few months. I am designated as a "House Mouse" or put more basically one of a few selected recruits to be slaves to the DIs for the duration. (Clean the platoon office, polish any brass in sight, shine the DIs boots & shoes, etc.) A new world awaits us all. We are called maggots, scum, girls, ladies, pussies and other less positive names to break us down from our preconceived thoughts of how great we each were. We are being molded into a cohesive unit of well-trained fighting machines. Our Drill Instructors (DIs) are to be our mother, father, sister, girlfriend, or whatever; in other words, they are our lifeline for the next 12 weeks of pure hell. The rules are simple whatever your DI says is gospel, no questioning his authority, you just do it and do it NOW! We are informed that for the next eight weeks we will see no one other than our fellow recruits; no visitors, no phone calls, unless a family emergency happens. The rule is you can have visitors after you return from rifle range training.

The next morning, we first got haircuts, or shall I say our heads were shaved of all remnants of hair. My childhood crewcuts would have been considered being of the long-haired hippy verity in comparison. One poor young recruit with shoulder length hair was crying as he was shorn of his golden locks. The DI's of course screamed at him for being a cry-baby. We discovered that he was in real pain since beneath his long hair he had had a mole that the shears cut through and his head was coated in blood. That was definitely a very painful event for him.

That day we removed all of our civilian attire and were issued our initial training uniforms which consisted of boxer shorts, t-shirt, sweat socks, white tennis shoes, green utility trousers, a yellow sweatshirt with the

Marine Corps emblem on the front (we spray painted our names on the back with a stencil), a utility cover (never referred to as a hat) and a web belt that flopped down your leg after putting on since it was too long.

November 12: Our training commences - 12 weeks of pure and meticulous hell whose objective is to mold us into a cohesive unit of battle-ready Marines. The first week is consumed with issuing uniforms, medical examinations, inoculations (even though I had recently returned from Japan and had incurred a 23-inoculation battery before transit the doctors ignored my shot record and commenced to give me a new battery of them), dental examinations and dental work. I personally believe that the Navy Dentists were using us recruits for experimentation of new techniques and/or amalgams for filing cavities. Before entering the Marines, my teeth were my pride and joy with only one cavity in my seventeen years. After the Boot Camp Dental work I had a filling in the majority of my teeth. I remember visiting my old family dentist on my first leave after boot camp and Dr. Claire asked me what happened to my teeth. He was astonished at the number of fillings that he said were covering almost every one of my molars on more than one surface, top, side, etc. I hope that the use of my formerly strong teeth for experimentation helped advance the dental capability of the Navy doctors. During our first week we are issued our weapons and field equipment, instructed in the proper care and grooming of the ice plants surrounding our Quonset huts. God forbid if some poor soul broke a single leaf on the sacred ice plants. He would then have to carefully place sand against the broken leaf to hold it in place so no one would notice the damage. During this week we also began most of our initial introduction to close order drill, care of our rifle, laundry, writing home, etc. Yes, we were expected to write home every week and tell our family and friends how wonderfully we were being treated. We also learned the rules of the smoking lamp. When the order, "The smoking lamp is lit for ONE cigarette!" each of us were expected to light up and enjoy a relaxing smoke. If you weren't a smoker you soon learned how. If anyone lit a second cigarette or smoked after the smoking lamp was extinguished the whole platoon suffered dearly. I must let you know of the first (and thankfully the last) time one of our platoon broke (or got caught breaking) the smoking rules. Our DI called us to formation and marched us to the end of our platoon street to a large trash dumpster and ordered us to climb in. Once inside he had us each light up a cigarette and then closed to top. We heard him yell, "INHALE, HOLD, EXHALE" about four times before opening the dumpster. Needless to say there was a bunch of green around the gills boots scrambling out of that dumpster choking and gasping for air. The word was spread by our leaders that if anyone lit up again without permission there was sure to be a "Blanket Party" held in the middle of the night for discipline. A blanket party was a ritual beating performed by your fellow recruits while your sheet and blanket were held tightly over you so you couldn't get out of your bunk. Thus began our guidance and discipline that was to eventually mold us into a cohesive unit of Marines.

Second week 11-18-63: We are now getting into our schedule of rifle instruction, close order drill and classes on Marine Corps and United States Military History. Midday Monday a company runner comes to our platoon area with a message for our DI, "Costanza has visitors at the visitor center." The DI sends him back with a message that we are not allowed visitors yet. The runner returns with the following message "Lt. Col. Hunter has received permission from base commander Major General Hochmuth to visit recruit Costanza and he expects Costanza there immediately." I am told to put on my best starched utility uniform and report to the visitor center and cautioned not to eat any pogeybait (a slang term for any delicious food not from the mess hall). I report to the visitor center and am greeted by Lt. Col. and Mrs. Hunter and their daughter Anita (she was always beautiful but today she seemed to glow). Ah, finally a touch of reality and the outside world. Of course, I enjoy a hamburger and large order of fries with a delicious Coca-Cola. Half an hour later I return to our platoon area. Our DI screams "Mount up", which means we are going on a little hike with full marching pack. The pace is fast and about fifteen minutes into the hike I step to the side of the trail and heave my guts out. My DI says, "That's what pogeybait will do to you, get back in formation." The pace was slowed as we returned to our Quonset huts to get ready for dinner (real food my DI noted). Another lesson is learned; your DI is always right about proper eating habits.

11 A.M. Friday November 22: We are called into the base theater for a company muster. An officer goes to the podium and says, "Marines, I have some information to relay to you." We all looked at each other

and realized that it must be something big for us Boot Camp scum to be called Marines before completing our training. The news was BIG; President John F. Kennedy had been assassinated and we are the first to know of his death. Our schedule is changed; we are to go to rifle range (Camp Matthews) immediately to learn to fire our weapons because if Latin America blows up we will be the first sent. Welcome to the reality of being in the Marines who are the first to fight in any "police" action the government starts. Later in the day that change in schedule was to be rescinded and training returned to normal but we all were aware of the fact that the world around us had just changed significantly. The most significant thing I remember is getting back to our platoon area and our DIs telling us to blouse our trousers. This is a way of announcing to the other new recruits that we were moving closer to being officially Marines. If one screws up he may be told to un-blouse his trousers as a sign of failure. Platoon 287 was the first of our series to be told to blouse their trousers and not one of us lost that privilege. We were aiming for perfection and status as a Regimental Honor Platoon. As usual our weekly tests are superior to the rest of the series and Platoon 287 wins a ribbon for our colors.

Third week 11-25-63: Swimming instruction and testing are on tap for this week. We learn how to jump properly off the side of a ship feet first, remove our trousers while treading water and turn them into pretty efficient water wings. We are also introduced to the conditioning course which included:
- swinging on a rope over a water hazard
- inclined rail fence climbing
- vertical wall climb
- rope net climbing (getting from ship to landing craft)
- rope climb
- stump jumping (balance conditioning)
- final rope, ladder beam walk, wall climb and descent

Fourth week 12-02-63: After a week of basic conditioning we embark on the endurance course with log drills ending in a combat readiness test on Friday. The endurance course is an enhanced version of the confidence course with more difficult arm and hand hanging maneuvers and log drills. The log drills required eight recruits to do arm presses of a telephone pole while lying on their back, tossing said telephone pole above their heads and catching it several times. The eight-man team must have good comradeship and coordination to maintain the cadence counted out by the DI. Finally, we end the week with the Combat Readiness Test (CRT). The CRT is a repeat of much of the aforementioned tests plus the fireman's carry and other new challenges. The CRT is also done with field marching pack and rifles to add to the difficulty while building combat readiness skills. The CRT is competition for our series and, as usual, Platoon 287 is the best and earns another banner.

Fifth week 12-09-63: Happy 18th birthday recruit Costanza. We are now coming together as a more cohesive unit working constantly with our rifles in hand. We do physical drill under arms which literally means we exercise while using our weapons as tools. We hold them outstretched for extended periods of time thrust them in cadence with our instructors' commands. Our weapons become an extension of our bodies, an integral part of who we are

Sixth week 12-16-63: We spend much of our sixth week working on physical fitness, pushups, pull-ups squat thrusts, sit-ups, etc. Week six ends in a Physical Readiness Test for the series and, as usual, Platoon 287 is the best and earns another banner.

Seventh week 12-23-63: By now we are confident about are abilities and spend time readying ourselves for our first major inspection. We shine our boots, polish our brass, starch and iron our uniforms, block our covers and most importantly put many hours into cleaning and cleaning and then cleaning again our rifles for inspection. Wednesday is Christmas which means a day off from our regular schedule. Corporal Cothran being the most junior DI is assigned to (as he called it) "baby sit" 287. His unhappiness with the assignment is borne out through his emphasis on our constantly drilling on the grinder. We march past the base chapel while Christmas services are being held and sing loudly to his cadence a newly learned Christmas carol: Jingle bells, jingle bells privates in the grass, take your merry Christmas tree and shove it up your ass." Needless to say, the attendees at the service were not impressed by our wonderful lyrics. We spent the rest of Christmas day doing calisthenics and cleaning up our platoon area to prepare for our end of week inspection. Passing the seventh week inspection means we are ready to move on to Camp Matthews for rifle range and small arms training once again Platoon 287 is the best and earns another banner.

Eighth week 12-30-63: On to Camp Matthews for Rifle Range. The beginning of two weeks of marksmanship training and infantry field skills then rifle qualification. Our PMI (Personnel Marksmanship Instructor) seems to treat us better than our DI, he needs us to learn and learn quickly how to shoot our rifles properly. We soon find out that there are two very special hills here at Camp Matthews appropriately name Big Agony and Little Agony. Little Agony is a "small" hill that we run up and down with full pack carrying our rifles at full arm's length to bolster our endurance. Big Agony on the other hand is the ultimate test of our endurance, at least 4 times as large as its little sister "Big Agony" is where we learn to "listen" very carefully to orders. We stand at the bottom in formation with our sea bags fully loaded as our PMI barks, "Pick up your shit and run to the top." We all grab our sea bags and run full tilt up this steep "hill." The first squad to the top waves their pendant and the PMI screams, "First squad, come back down." We run back down and fall in only to be asked, "Who told you to bring those bags down with you take them back up and report to me in formation." This time we run up and leave our sea bags on the top of the hill as ordered. This routine of running up and down "Big Agony" continues for several hours until all of us are near exhaustion. We are being taught that to be a cohesive unit we must listen to "exactly" what orders are being given and to respond immediately (no questions asked) as a team.

Ninth week 01-06-64: This week I get a surprise visitor, my dad is back in the States in California and comes to Camp Matthews to say hello. He lets me know how proud he is of me and my success in Boot Camp. He sends me a letter from his motel that I receive the next day and I get pretty choked up to know how proud he is of me. My Di allows me time alone in my tent to compose myself before reporting back to training. I guess they have hearts after all. Neither my Di nor my PMI made any comments on how I reacted to dad's visit and letter but of course they knew he was a retired Mustang so his expressing pride in me reflected on their superior training abilities.

Our Drill Instructors supplement the intense regimen of strict compliance to any and all orders to help us to be quick to respond in any situation. We become more and more aware of the necessity of unfaltering teamwork. We learn the mechanics of our weapons, each of us can strip down our rifles and reassemble them in under a minute (in the dark), and we are now ready to learn how to fire them. More practice on triangulation (using wooden rifles), remember your BRASS (Breathe, Relax, Aim, Slack, Squeeze), making and marking targets in the butts, 45 caliber pistol training, semi-automatic rifle on bipod. The pressure to qualify is intense, a week of practice and then Pre-Qual Day and Qualification Day. I Pre-Qualify as an expert marksman but the next day is foggy and the mist plays tricks on one's aim. Most of us qualify lower than the day before. I just qualify as a Marksman but I qualified. One member of another platoon scored so low on the first two firing lines that even with a perfect score on the last he would not qualify. He goes to the alibi shed (a small shed near the final firing line where poor shooters go to commiserate with each other on their inability to shoot) on the way back to the last line and blows his brains out. His fellow platoon members are given the task to clean up after him. I guess some people fail and cannot live with it. It is a sad day for us but tomorrow is another day of long hikes and training. We must remain focused on our goal to finish Boot Camp and to become Marines. Platoon 287 is superior to the others in our series so, as usual, we get another banner to attach to our colors. We head back to MCRD Sand Diego for our last week and a half before graduation.

Tenth week 01-13-64: We are on the final lap of our journey to become Marines. We learn hand to hand combat on the bayonet course with pugil stick training. The pugil stick is a long wooden pole with padding on both ends like a giant Q-tip. One end has a stripe around it to designate the bayonet end. We have competition between platoons to see who is best. I am the last of 287 to compete and my opponent is the largest (an almost 300-pound black marine) member of the other platoon. He pretty much wants to destroy me and claim the honor of his platoon and win the final banner. As he starts to charge at me with his pugil stick pointed at my head I crouch down and set my stick at a 45-degree angle and bring the butt end up between his legs. His momentum allows me to lift him off the ground and throw him out of the circle. I claim victory for 287 and once again we earn a ribbon. We spend the next couple of days on a final overnight bivouac. We finish the week with clothing alterations (class A uniforms for graduation).

Eleventh week 01-20-64: Our platoon wins many (translated as ALL) honors for our excellence. We always run in formation with the tallest in front and the shortest pulling up the rear eating the others dust. Monday during the final Physical Readiness Test (PRT) one of the lead recruits, 6'6" Joe L. Jones falls to the ground. Petey Moore and I (the two shortest) grab Joe under the arms and begin dragging him to the finish line (we always finish with all 100% succeeding) to keep our record perfect. Our Junior DI Corporal Cothran runs by, looks at Joe and says, "Drop him he's dead." Shocked but dutiful to orders we leave Joe behind and run to finish with the rest of the platoon. We come to find out that Joe had a heart condition and died because of it. The other Platoon Drill Instructors argued that we shouldn't receive the 100% ribbon because Joe failed to complete the final PRT. They lost that argument so we maintained our perfect record.

January 22, 1964: Graduation Day - We are now officially Marines. Our platoon chants, "287 is shoveling shit, the rest of the series is eating it." We are

the Regimental Honor Platoon. We have won every competition and earned all the banners. No one is better than we are.

Next on the agenda is six weeks of Advanced Infantry Training (AIT) at Camp Pendleton. There we learn about many facets of combat and weaponry; We learn how to dig a foxhole with our entrenching tools, to "enjoy" c-rations in the middle of a hot, dry desert training session, map reading and finding your way using a compass at night. We have the thrill of crawling under barbed wire with live machinegun fire whizzing over our butts and small dynamite charges exploding in craters to our left and right. We train with Browning Automatic Rifles, machine guns (M-60's, 50 cals), grenades (rifle and hand thrown), Bangalore torpedoes, mines, flamethrowers, 60mm mortars, ¼ sticks of dynamite, and 3.5" rocket launchers among other equipment.

During Advanced Infantry Training we see the humorous side of our instructors. While learning how to set ¼ sticks of dynamite for explosion we take a blasting cap and wire with crimpers in one hand and the dynamite in another, place them behind our backs, slip the blasting cap into the dynamite stick and crimp the blasting cap and wire. If you were the second group to follow this procedure the instructor gave the order to crimp exactly the same time as the previous group's charges were set off. One can imagine what went through your mind as you crimped the blasting cap and heard a loud explosion simultaneously. The instructor quickly asked if anyone needed to go change their skivvies (what a wonderful sense of humor?). Hand grenade training was another thing altogether, we were matched up with individual trainers and got into foxholes dug into a cliff-top. The foxholes were wide enough for two people (the recruit & the trainer) with a hole in the bottom wide enough for an errant grenade to be kicked into in case of being dropped to allow it to explode without harming either Marine in the foxhole. If a grenade was accidentally dropped the trainer would yell, "Fire in the hole!" and all on the line would immediately take cover. If you were in a foxhole with your trainer, he would clasp his hands around your hands and grenade to prevent the spoon from being released and pull you down into the foxhole for protection. This happened once while we were training with terrible results. The young Marine was following the instructions (Hold the grenade with your right hand spoon in your palm and grasp the firing pin with your left, hold it to your chest, pull the pin, bring the grenade in your right hand to behind you right ear, throw the grenade over the cliff by pushing it forward quickly releasing the spoon as you throw) just as he moved the grenade to behind his ear he panicked and dropped it into the foxhole. His trainer yelled out, "Fire in the hole!" and tried to kick the grenade into the hole at the bottom but the scared recruit had his foot stuck in the hole. The trainer grabbed the grenade, pushed the recruit down and using a two-hand basketball throw tried to discard the grenade over the cliff. Unfortunately, the grenade went off as he released it and exploded in his face killing him. The recruit was so shaken up that he was given a section 8 (mental) discharge soon after the event.

One rather unnerving event was during training under live fire. The course had live machine gun fire 18 inches above our path. We had to crawl on our stomachs cradling our rifles while small explosive charges went off near us. The charges were in small mounds in our path so we couldn't be hurt by them but when one went off next to you it gave you quite a start. We were constantly reminded to keep our butts down since the machine gun fire was whizzing above us. I remember my helmet digging a through in the sand as I crawled from end to end of the course. All of a sudden there was a scream of pain then a command "Cease Firing keep your heads down and hug the dirt". We were instructed in which direction to face before standing up the led from the course being told to keep looking forward. We came to find out that one of the Marines on the course got spooked and stood up into the machine gun fire and was cut down immediately by the bullets. I can still hear the scream that occurred about five feet from me. The mounds of dirt shielding the explosive charges prevented me from seeing what happened but the sounds still reverberate whenever I think back to my Pendleton training days. Death comes quickly during training I thought promising myself to be even more attentive to training orders from then on until completing AIT.

Our first weekend liberty was given and a group of us went down to a local hangout near Pendleton for some entertainment. Most of us were underage so drinking was prohibited but (surprise) some older personnel found it in their hearts to provide us with some 3.2 beer. There was a comedienne performing that evening named Rusty Warren known for her raucous comedy. Her opening comment to a bunch of young Marines on their first escape from training was, "You guys are wonderful I would love to kiss everyone in the joint but I might get thrown out of here." We, of course, interpreted the word "joint" as a particular part of our anatomy and roared with laughter. A couple of weeks later we graduated from Advanced Infantry Training and were sent home for the first time.

I must now comment on my first trip home since joining the Marines. My family was still living on assignment in Japan so I went to visit my older sister who was living in Maryland. While back in my old stomping grounds I tried to visit an old girlfriend whom I had dated when living in Riverdale. Her father answered the door and noticed this young Marine (in uniform) at his door asking to see Penny. He wasn't exactly thrilled with the prospect of his young daughter (18 years old) going out with a military man and told me, "My daughter isn't allowed to go out with you because I know what you want. You only want to get into her pants." Actually, I just wanted to go out with some of my friends, but his suggestions did arouse some interest in my mind. I left his house confused but still ready to reconnect with old friends. Side note: Penny, I found out a little later, had become a "Playboy Bunny" in the Baltimore hutch. I met up with a couple of old buddies and found out that the CYO (Catholic Youth Organization) was having a dance the next evening. I decided to go and check out some ladies. Since I only had my uniforms I borrowed clothes from my friends (BIG mistake). The only clothes they had to spare were, a pair of Madras slacks, Madras shirt, Madras sport coat and Madras tie – none of which matched. I looked like an escapee from a Vaudeville show. I guess the fact that I was a Marine was enough for the girls to ignore my outfit as I had a wonderful time and danced with the cream of the crop all night long.

After that short leave at home with family it's on to the Naval Air Technical Training Center at Millington, Tennessee just outside of Memphis for Avionics School. I finish Basic Electronics and enter Aviation Fire Control RADAR School. I am partnered with Private Roberts for lab sessions. Both Roberts and I loved playing with electronics as we grew up so we excelled in our lab work. Our best accomplishment was building the best ever super-heterodyne receiver. The object was to use schematics given to us, an aluminum chassis (we needed to lay out all components and punch holes in it for sockets for tubes and other parts), and access to a large selection of parts to build our receiver. Roberts and I looked over the schematic given to us and made several modifications that we thought would enhance its capabilities. The final test of our project was to tune in as many AM stations as possible while keeping a log of each. Our receiver was capable of getting more than three times the number of stations as our nearest competitor even after our instructor found our hidden antennae (installed during a secret night maneuver) that went out the window and onto the roof. Inside our chassis we had added two push-pull amplifiers to enhance the signal going through our circuits. Our instructor was impressed by our design so we got the best grade possible (99% for Marines since only sailors could get 100%) for our project.

On one of our first liberty calls four of us stopped at the Millington Diner for lunch. We ordered hamburgers, fries and Coke. Three of us got our meals quickly while our black Marine friend wasn't served. When we asked where his meal was the waitress pointed to a sign that read," WE RESERVE THE RIGHT TO REFUSE SERVICE TO ANYONE." At that time the owner stuck his head out of the kitchen and screamed, "What is that NIGGER doing in my diner." Since we only saw four Marines we pushed our plates away from us and left without paying and returned to base. In the barracks we discussed with our fellow students (Marines and Sailors) about what had occurred and decided to take a stand. We put on our class "A" uniforms and returned in force to the diner filling every seat at the counter and all tables. We (the original four) sat in our same seats and our black comrade repeated our order with the same result, the black Marine was refused service. The owner then came out of the kitchen and confronted us. He asked what the hell we thought we were doing. We expressed our displeasure with his refusal to serve our black comrade and ask that he reconsider. He fumed back into the kitchen only to return a half hour later demanding that all the customers drinking only free water leave the premises. As we stood up we asked him to look out at his parking lot to see the line of Marines and Sailors ready to take our seats until our black comrade was served. He said he didn't really give a shit. After a couple of cycles of full tables ordering only water while one black Marine ordered lunch he came out of the kitchen again to ask us what we wanted. We told him we wanted our friend served, his sign removed and replaced with one stating, "We proudly serve ALL of our American servicemen." As he removed the offensive sign and fed our black comrade the rest of us sat down to a good lunch and I dare say not only did we make a breakthrough for racial equality in early 1964 but the diner owner probably had his most profitable day ever feeding the multitudes of Marines and Sailors waiting in line. The year 1964 was full of racial tension throughout the South. We once were called out on "dungaree liberty" and allowed to go into Memphis in our usually on-base only utility uniforms to assist the local police in quelling a potential race riot. We carried our unloaded weapons with scabbarded bayonets fixed in place down Beale Street to help push demonstrators into side streets in an attempt to calm down a tenuous situation. I recall at that time watching a wedge of police moving forward with a large German Shepard police dog in front towards the crowd of demonstrators. Suddenly the crowd opened a gap and one of the protestors stepped forward with a larger Doberman Pincer dog and let it loose at the German Shepard. The dog fight didn't last long as the police were able to separate the two dogs and take away the Doberman on a heavy-duty leash. The sixties were definitely a decade of racial stress and confrontation.

I did have several wonderful memories that year in Memphis. I was lured to the Arthur Murray Dance Studio by a couple of beautiful young southern belles for a couple of "free" dance lessons only to find out that the manager was using the ladies to bait servicemen into long term dance class contracts. During my second "free" lesson the manager pulled me aside and asked if I would like to earn some extra money on weekends teaching his female instructors how to dance several ballroom dances. It seems my abilities at the cha-cha, foxtrot, etc. were better than his ladies. So I was paid for several weekends to dance with the prettiest of the Memphis belles.

My favorite Memphis memory though was when a fellow Marine's girlfriend asked him if he had a couple friends on base to attend a birthday party and he asked me to go along. His girlfriend picked us up at the main gate and drove us to the party. We were shocked when the car drove into the gates of Graceland. We figured that the girl's family had rented a room there for her party. We did not know at the time that the girl's older sister knew Elvis personally due to attending high school with him. The party was held in a large room with comfortable living room furniture and a large fireplace. Our greatest surprise was when Elvis joined us in the room and sat there sharing Coca Colas with us. It took almost two hours for us to talk him into picking up his guitar and playing a couple of songs for us. As I recall Hound Dog, Love Me Tender, Blue Suede Shoes and Little Sister were four of the songs he sang. I believe that his agreeing to sing was due to the fact that there were four Marines in the room and he wanted to give us something to remember. I will always remember that party.

Finally, I graduated from NATTC Millington, Tennessee with a GPA of 98.6 as top Marine in my class. Being number one Marine I got choice of duty stations. There are 8 billets available one for El Toro, CA and the other 7 for Cherry Point, NC. California here I come

1965 Choice duty - El Toro, California - surf, sea and babes. Can life really get any better than this? I join VMFA 542 as an Aviation Fire Control Technician

responsible for the maintenance of the control system of the tiger's teeth, its missile guidance systems. The McDonnell Douglas F-4B Phantom II was equipped with a compliment of two radar systems, the Westinghouse

APQ-72 pulse radar (an X-band air-search radar) and the Raytheon APA-157 CW radar (Sparrow missile control) and an infrared sensing system, the Texas Instruments AAA-4 IRST (Infra-Red Search & Track) pod (Sidewinder missile control) under the nose. When I arrived at El Toro the APQ-72 radar system modulator/demodulator (M/D) unit was comprised of miniature (peanut) vacuum tubes. In late February we received the first all transistorized M/D unit that I, being the newest and junior member of the RADAR shop, was assigned to install. Of course, the new connector at the end of the cable going to the transistorized unit was different than the existing cable connector. This meant crawling into the radome and cutting the large cable that went from the aircraft wiring harness to the M/D unit and splicing each individual wire while chasing down each to assure every signal went to the correct pin. Several hours later I crawl out of the radome and we check out the new unit. Much to my pleasure there were no wiring errors. I really didn't want to crawl back into the radome and bake for a couple more

We are briefed on an upcoming exercise, "Operation Silver Lance", a training exercise to set up a temporary

airfield on San Clemente Island located off the coast of southern California. This operation was to have lasted from 23 February through 10 March 1965. So VMFA 542 (the Fighting Tigers) headed to Port Hueneme as part of "Operation Silver Lance", We then boarded the USS Alamo, which is a LSD (Landing Ship Dock – a flat bottomed piece of crap), and head west. We were to soon find out that the USS Alamo was being called upon to make an unscheduled run to Yokosuka carrying men and equipment for the American military buildup in the Far East as the United States was beginning direct participation in operations in Vietnam. Ten days later, still heading west and nowhere near San Clemente Island our officer in charge reads us our sealed orders. We were en route to Da Nang, Vietnam. We asked ourselves where the hell was Vietnam and why were we going there? My classmates at Cherry Point were leaving on a Med Cruise to Rota, Spain. We soon found out the answer. A small group of wet behind the ears Marines who did not have a clue of what was coming next took to sea. Gung Ho and Semper Fi were our cries. The LSD in not exactly the type of boat one enjoys traveling the "Great Circle Route" from California to Japan via the Aleutian Islands area. We see every conceivable kind of weather on our trip; a water spout nearby, heavy rain, fog, snow, sleet and huge ocean swells as we pray we stay on top of the water. During one especially stormy night where the seas were rolling huge, the rain was heavy and stinging my face as I stood port watch on deck. The fog was so thick that you couldn't see your fingers on your outstretched hand. The comes a rather intelligent (?) shout from the Lieutenant JG in the pilot house, "Port guard we have a radar contact at five miles can you give me a visual?" I replied, "Sir, in this weather if the Queen Mary crossed our bow with all lights on at that distance I couldn't give you a visual" He wasn't too pleased at my response. During my short break between port and starboard watches in the pilot house I was looking at a u-shaped glass tube mounted on the wall. It was contained an air bubble that showed the angle the ship's hull was in the water. There were two marks at around 45 degrees on either side that the bubble seemed to rock back and forth between. The officer said that if the bubble went higher than either mark the ship wasn't guaranteed to stay upright. Watching the bubble slide past one or the other mark in particularly rough seas was a strange feeling as the ship bounced down the side of the wave it was cresting. Each time we gave out a sigh of relief that we bounced rather than tipped. As the weather cleared we all felt more relaxed. As we approached the Japanese coast one of my fellow Marines made less than complimentary comments about the Japanese people specifically the women whom he described as nothing but a bunch of whores looking to take our money. Since I had spent my senior year of High School at Misawa Air Force base in Japan I gave him a piece of my mind. We crossed the Pacific landing at the United States Navy base, in Yokosuka, Japan then heading to Atsugi Naval Air Station, Japan to wait for our aircraft to arrive. We arrived at Yokosuka, off-loaded our equipment then went by caravan to NAS Atsugi to prepare for the arrival of our aircraft. By the way the wise-ass who spoke badly of the Japanese people eventually went home with an oriental bride – go figure.

We travel from Japan to Vietnam (via the Philippines) on the USS Vernon County, a LST (Landing Ship Transport - a smaller ship that normally carries landing craft and troops not aircraft equipment). As we enter the South China Sea we watch the sailors  prepare to test their guns as we enter a combat zone. The drill is to test your guns by firing a couple of rounds and watching their splash to verify accuracy. Four of us marines were on deck playing pinochle as the Chief Petty Officer in charge of the nearest gun turret prepared for the test. Just then some brilliant soul (a blowhard Lieutenant JG) demands he be the one to be in charge. The Chief protests but is told "If anyone is going to fire the first rounds from our ship it will be me." The chief explains the procedure and is told, "I am a Naval Academy graduate and I don't need to be schooled by you." The Chief asks us to be witness to his turning over command of his gun mount then lets the Lt JG take over. The JG fires two test rounds from the twin 3"/50 over the horizon so we see NO splash. Unfortunately, the rounds flew across the bow of the USS Enterprise (radio silence kept us from knowing they were nearby). We watch as 4 McDonnell Douglass F4B Phantom II aircraft (fully loaded for combat) cross our bow to check us out. Following the F4B inspection a helicopter lands on our fantail and out steps an officer with more "scrambled eggs" (the nickname for the golden oak leaf embellishments on the peaks of dress hats worn by officer personnel in the grade of major/O-4 or higher in the Army and Marine Corps, and officer personnel in the grade of commander/O-5 or higher in the Navy and Coast Guard) on his cover than I had ever seen before. He was an Admiral from the carrier along with his Lt JG lackey. We all stood at attention as he inquired as to who was responsible for the two rounds just fired. The Lt JG was singled out by those of us on deck as the "person in charge of the mount." The admiral proceeded to read him the riot act stating that the two rounds he fired landed about 500 yards from the Enterprise and that if the Enterprise had been going a few more knots faster the rounds would have hit their flight deck full of aircraft and personnel. Guess which Lt JG is removed and sent stateside to the brig waiting for courts marshal and whose lackey is told to remain on our ship to relieve him? The Admiral's Lt JG admin wasn't too happy about his change in status and warned the exiting Lt JG, "If I ever see you stateside outside of the brig I will kill you. You screwed me out of a cushy job with the Admiral asshole." We keep pressing onward toward our destiny.

July 10, 1965 - South China Sea, Republic of Vietnam: We sit on deck watching sheets of tracer round crisscross the beach where we are to land at 0530 tomorrow. Another couple hands of pinochle and hearts are played then we hit the rack knowing that when we wake up we will be heading to shore (finally solid land). We awake for morning muster and wait for touch of land. Our first daylight view of Vietnam filled us with awe at the beauty of the crystal-clear water and almost white sand lined with plush greenery. The beach had been secured during the night by our fellow Marines. A line of 4-bys wait for us on shore. We offload our equipment into the waiting vehicles and fall in. The first call I hear is "Costanza, shotgun truck number two". I am issued loaded magazines for my rifle and report to the second vehicle then hop into the cab in the passenger's seat. The driver is as young as I am but looks older and hardened due to his time in the war. We start toward Da Nang (a two-hour drive according to the Motor-T guy driving). Twenty minutes later the first vehicle pulls to the side of the road. "What the FUCK?" the driver says, "Don't tell me his engine overheated again. Costanza, go up and see what's wrong". I walk up to the lead truck (the others are passing by us to keep moving on) to ask what the problem is. My friend (whom shall remain nameless but was another air-dale who "volunteered" to ride shotgun) looked rather pale and was holding his rifle against his helmet in a death grip and shaking. I looked to the driver for help but half his face and the back of his head were plastered onto the rear wall of the cab. "WELCOME TO VIETNAM." I thought. Not more than a half hour on land and I realized that this was a real war and I was there whether I liked it or not.

I let my driver know what has happened and he radios for a replacement driver from one of the trucks at the end of the column. "I guess we're going to have to finally send a fire team after that sniper." he says "He's been firing at us here for weeks but never hit more than the dirt around us, either he has learned to shoot better or there is someone new out there. The grunts will have him gone by evening."

I learn that they would rather leave a poor sniper alone until he kills someone rather than waste time taking him out and having him replaced by a real sharp shooter. War is strange, I thought, you play mind games with yourself and the enemy and pray you don't get tagged. The rest of the trip was long and hot, the driver said it was a rather cool day. Cool my ass I thought, you could fry eggs on the hood of his truck. After a couple hours of driving through small villages and the city of Da Nang, we finally arrive at our destination, the wonderful garden apartments of the Marine tent camp area. We unload our equipment and settle into our new home away from home.

And so began a tour of the beautiful country of Vietnam. I truly mean beautiful country, when we arrived in early 1965 the land was plush with green foliage and the beach from Da Nang to Chu Lai was 55 miles of the cleanest sand with deep blue crystal-clear water that you loved to relax in whenever you had the chance (not often). The people were wonderful and the women were gorgeous. I enjoyed going into town to have a cool (warm maybe) beer at a local bar and meeting the people. We were not allowed to take our weapons with us when we went into Da Nang (funny in a war zone don't you think) to prevent incidents. I checked my rifle at the gate as I left base (I did have my bayonet safely tucked in my boot and a 22P Berretta in a shoulder holster under my left arm – who knew but me?) to head into Da Nang. That Beretta would come in handy later in this tour. Contrary to what we were told in preparation for our tour the local food choices (steak sandwiches made from either monkey or dog available at the airport cafe) were excellent and the local beer passable (in more ways than one - the sign of the Tiger makes you go go go). They had a local beer with a Tiger on the bottle that tasted like crap but you could get a quick buzz off a liter or two. I had a couple of specific bars I frequented most and got to know the Vietnamese people pretty well. They were a hard-working people with great pride in their country and a love for the land. I worked with the local orphanage when I had time off and a liberty pass. A few of us also volunteered to ride shotgun on RVN Army helicopters (our weapons were semi-automatic and the RVN's weren't) to assist in pulling local villagers out of the way of approaching Viet Cong (VC). We'd pick up the women, children and old men bring to a safe place and after the Viet Cong finished leveling their village we brought them back to their village. We then helped them rebuild their huts and restart their lives all the time knowing that if we failed to return to Da Nang on time for duty we would be classified as AWOL and/or listed as MIA. We just felt it our duty to help the people survive.

I believe that on one of those flights something happened that I keep locked out of my memories that my dreams (nightmares) forever refuse to let go of. The following is an excerpt from my journal of the early nineties when I was working with Rev. Dr. Robert Stoudt on analyzing some of my dreams and/or nightmares that were causing me stress and thoughts of suicide as my second marriage was falling apart:

"I must fight alone, no reinforcements, no armor, just me, just like the time in the jungle, a helicopter above and me down below shooting at anything that moved. My escape route closed by my own personal barrage only in the war I ran out of ammo and was pulled home to safety by my friends. What happened in the jungle? Did I kill my own friends? God help me to remember, help me to make amends. Why did the pilot stay up there and leave me alone? I don't remember I was only told about what they saw from above; I was shooting into the jungle at something or someone. It was unsafe for them to land. What did I do that was so terrible that my mind refuses to let remember? Did I really hold someone in my arms as they died? Was it all a dream or a horror too painful to face?"

It was at my favorite bar that my Berretta Pistol came in handy. A friend and I had stopped in for a couple of cold beers. My buddy went into the back room with his favorite "girlfriend" while I sat and talked with the waitress. All of a sudden, this VC walks in with a grenade in his hand looking to blow a few Marines up. When he turned his back to me and walked towards the back room I put my Berretta behind his right ear, cocked it and grabbed his arm. I yelled to my buddy in pig Latin "Am-scray" explaining the situation so the locals didn't understand what I was saying. I heard him jump through the window and leave as I stood there with an idiot and a grenade in my sights. I asked the bartender to explain to the VC asshole that I intended to blow his brains out if he didn't hand me the grenade without pulling the pin. It seemed like an eternity but eventually he gave the grenade to me. The bartender told me that the young woman in the back room was the VC's cousin and he wasn't happy with her consorting with Americans. I had the bartender tell the VC to get the hell out of town before I lose my cool and put a hole in his fucking head. He ran out of the bar and disappeared. My decision to not kill him was mainly one of self-preservation, not wanting to have to explain my actions or my having a hidden pistol on me while on liberty. I reconnoiter with my buddy and we return to base ready to fight another day.

I must tell you now of a wonderful weekend I had while on liberty. One of the RVN officers I rode shotgun for thanked me for my help by telling me to go to a certain area of DaNang and look for a Pedi-cab driver with a patch over his right eye and ask him to take me to the "estate." The "estate" I found out was an old French villa where a pair of gorgeous Vietnamese twins lived. The driver dropped me off Saturday morning and said he would return for me Sunday afternoon. I wasn't sure what to expect but I soon found out. Those lovely ladies invited me in and asked me what I liked to drink. Being emboldened I said "Scotch" and one of them left the room and returned with a wonderful bottle of Chivas Regal and poured me a drink. They led me to a room with a large walk-in bath that looked more like a small swimming pool and told me to get undressed and relax in the warm water. I did as I was ordered and sat there sipping Chivas Regal and enjoying a relaxing bath. The two of them disrobed and joined me to carefully bathe me with soft sponges and to give me a full body massage. The rest of my visit with the two young women I will leave to your imagination but suffice to say I left on Sunday feeling wonderfully thanked by the RVN officer for my assistance with relocating people in danger. I never did see that Pedi-cab driver in town again, but I will never forget how the Vietnamese people could say thanks.

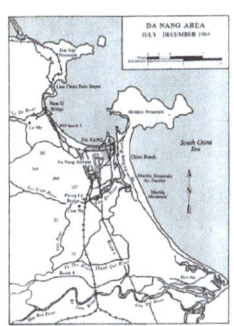

August 18, 1965 – Operation Starlite (also called the Battle of Chu Lai) is launched. Operation Starlite was the first major offensive regimental size action conducted by a purely U.S. military unit during the Vietnam War. The operation was conducted as a combined arms assault involving ground, air and naval units. U.S. Marines were deployed by helicopter insertion into the designated landing zone while an amphibious landing was used to deploy other Marines. Our F-4's dropped cluster bombs, resulting in an avalanche on the hillside which wiped out many of the attacking Viet Cong rifle and mortar squads. My clearest recollection was of six consecutive days that the nighttime was brighter than the daytime due to the thousands of flares dropped from KC-130's to light the ground below. The goal of protecting the air base at Chu Lai was a success. During Operation Starlite I pulled a weekend of guard duty (Friday August 20 – Sunday August 22). On guard duty at Da Nang you get the privelege of sleeping on the hard cots in the cells (with the doors open thank God). It makes one think before doing something stupid enough to get you put there with the door closed and locked. My second shift was from 0330 Saturday – 0730 Saturday. I went to my assigned post and looked for the person I was to relieve. He was lying on the ground against a wall with a cigarette buring between his fingers (I could smell his flesh burning.) He had a bullet hole between his eyes and half his brains were splattered on the wall where he had been standing. I reached into my pocket for my cigarettes to calm my nerves but could not light up. The thought of a sniper nearby looking for the burning ember as I took a drag was enough to make me crumble up the pack and throw them away it was at 0337 August 21st 1965 that I gave up smoking. I haven't smoked a cigarette since that night.

Another opportunity came to me from an Austrailian bush pilot flying spotter aircraft out of the civilian airfield at Da Nang. On one beautiful weekend he offered to take me for a ride to view the countryside from the air. Of course that wasn't exactly approved by the U. S. military so I was taking a big chance just as I did with the rescue missions, but I was intrigued to see the war zone from the air. The flight allowed me to see the utter distruction of the countryside (meaning foliage) caused by our C-123 fleet dropping Agent Orange to clear the jungle of vegetation. The lush landscape I previously viewed as breathtakingly beautiful was now withered and suffering to survive. I had seen aircraft from Da Nang flying near the base spraying defoliants but didn't think much about it until this close-up view from the air. I felt a deep dispair for the country I thought we were there to help but didn't talk about what I had observed so as to not admit flying illegaly with my Aussie friend. Those images stayed with me for a long time and disturbed my sleep at times. The sight of such distruction will never leave me and even as I write this memoir I feel sick to my stomach at what our presence in Vietnam did to not only the people but their beautiful land. I think that flight opened my eyes to the uselessness of war. But I digress from my writing so I return to my recollections.

One of the best uses of an F4B in Vet Nam was as a beer cooler. We had a brand-new centerline fuel tank that had never been used so we convinced one of our pilots to fly it to Saigon and try to have it filled with draft beer. He was successful and returned to Da Nang. As he pulled up on the tarmac a bunch of thirsty Marines greeted his aircraft with canteens and screwdrivers to "check" the centerline tank. Normally one would place a container under a small valve at the bottom of the tank and with a screwdriver push the valve and sample the fuel for water. On this occasion of course, the centerline tank spewed forth rather cool draft beer. Whenever we noticed that the beer was getting too warm we would fire up the aircraft and our pilot would take it up to over 10,000 feet long enough to cool down the beer. That was definitely the best day on the flight line.

On Friday evenings we would gather on a small field near the perimeter of base and watch movies on an outdoor screen. Of particular interest was the fact that the movie "El Cid" came in two canisters so it was shown on successive Fridays. For some reason during the second half we heard the call, "Incoming!" which meant the VC were firing mortars at us so the film was stopped and we dove for cover. Since films rotate around the bases it was a month before El Cid returned to Da Nang. When we got to the same part of the second half we once again heard the cry, "Incoming" and shut the film down and took cover. This happened once more before we figured that some VC was a film critic and we never reordered El Cid.

On one particular day I was returning from lunch at the civilian airport cafe when I heard a loud explosion and saw something streak down the runway past me. I metal object landed a couple of feet from me and I went over to pick it up. It was a circular clasp that was used to hold a sidewinder missile onto a rack mounted below the wing of an F4B. I went onto the runway to see what had happened and discover a streak from one of our aircraft down the tarmac where the missile had travelled. It ended its travels stuck into a sandbag bunker in the RVN Air Force Ordinance tent. The officer at the desk was frozen in place looking at the missile wondering if it was going to explode. A couple of members of our Ordinance Shop came by and removed it after assuring the officer that it couldn't have exploded since it didn't reach the proper speed to arm itself. It seems that one of our aircraft returned with an ordinance problem and the technicians were checking out the port missile rack not realizing that there was one sidewinder missile still mounted on the farthest starboard rack. As the test equipment went through the tests the system the cockpit display showed indicators from left to right "missile gone" until it found the last rack and fired the remaining missile that was heat sensor locked onto a piece of running equipment across the tarmac. I understand that at least 23 aircraft suffered minor shrapnel damage from the errant missile. The mishap earned itself a place in our Cruise Book as a comic sketch.

A short aside, "Nothing is more disconcerting than standing buck naked in an outdoor shower and looking across a muddy swamp to see several Viet Cong slithering through the weeds." Fortunately, our perimeter guards noticed them also and dispatched them rather quickly. Ah early morning Viet Nam style, never a dull moment.

1966 I volunteer for second tour at Da Nang - the people there really need our help! 52 crazy Marines volunteer to join a new squadron in transit to Vietnam;

they are fresh from the States and need experienced personnel to show them the ropes of being in a combat zone. Our new executive officer (XO) holds muster with us to welcome us to VMFA 314 "The Black Knights." His first comments are less than heartwarming: "You assholes think you are so wonderful because you volunteered to join our squadron. Well, you are NOT Black Knights and we do not need or appreciate your help. So help me God I will have each of you up in front of me within the first month of our tour and stripes will fall." I thought, "For this jerk we volunteered to go back into hell. Forgive me for not feeling welcome."

Our XO proved true to his word, by the end of our first month 51 of us had been busted for various bullshit charges from failing to salute an officer (hard to do while holding a radar antenna while someone bolts it in place) to being 5 minutes late to muster. The XO had a real hard-on for us salty Flying Tigers. We finally had the shits of the jerk so we decided to show him all the respect he requested. Effective immediately the Flying Tigers would each snap to attention whenever the XO approached and give him the snappiest salute we could muster. His overblown ego ate that shit up until one of his fellow officers asked him why he was so pleased with us setting him up as a target. His friend explained that if a VC sniper was observing our snappy saluting he would assume that the officer being saluted must be very important or of great rank. Ah, revenge would be sweet if our resident sniper kissed the asshole goodbye for us. After that conversation our XO made a point of avoiding running into any of the old Flying Tigers. He even held a muster in a closed hanger with us to request that we stop saluting him immediately, to which we all replied that we were not taking any chances with being busted again so we would keep up our diligence until we leave Viet Nam. This wonderful plan kept us free from his harassment for the remainder of our tour. There was also an RIO (Radar Intercept Officer) that flew back seat in the CO's F4B that was a pain in our asses by targeting the "Flying Tiger volunteers". This led to my greatest prank ever while in country. My fellow Flying Tiger's gave me much kudos and drowned me in gallons of beer to celebrate. I guess I wasn't very happy about being screwed when I volunteered to return to Da Nang and support a new squadron by not only being targeted for being busted but also by being put in Flight Line rather than Radar (my MOS). Graduating with a 98.9 average as top in my class from NATTC Millington I expected to remain in

Aviation Fire Control work my whole career not shoved into a different MOS by a new squadron that hated the "salty" Marines who showed a real can-do attitude by volunteering to serve another tour at war.

The 52 "misfits" were soon to realize how many crappy assignments could be dished out by a resident "asshole-in-charge." If there was a head to be drained of effluence, a late-night guard shift, long term mess duty or any one of myriad shitty tasks one of us would be assigned to accomplish the task. On one particular evening as a friend and I pulled a long shift of guard duty near our tent camp area to watch the perimeter we heard what we thought was digging and scraping beneath us. We walked the area near our post and found the source of the noise beneath us and marked it with a couple of stones. After repeated nights of hearing the noises and marking their position we noticed that we could draw a line from a specific building in the small village outside our perimeter and (following the stone markers) see that the target was to dig a tunnel underneath our fuel pits. We sat in the Enlisted Man's Club the next day and planned our course of action. We acquired a motorized posthole digger and when the digging started at the end nearest our fuel pits we quickly dug a posthole into the end of the tunnel near our perimeter and tossed in a couple of grenades. The tunnel collapsed and whoever was doing the digging was trapped underground forever. We sent a grunt patrol into the village to find the entrance of the tunnel and make sure it was destroyed. The couple of unfortunate VC who were captured in the village got to visit their deceased comrades that night thanks to swift justice handed out by the grunts. That same guard post was where I and a couple of comrades witnessed a young girl (about 8 or 9 years old) approach four Marines returning to Marble Mountain and put her hand out to beg for food. As the Marines reached in their packs for some c-rations to share we heard her say, "My mother said to give this to you." as she pulled a grenade from under here shirt and pulled the pin killing herself and injuring the four Marines.

My greatest prank: I was assigned as plane captain on the CO's aircraft while it was on hot pad duty. The drill was that each flight crew pre-flight their aircraft before reporting to hot pad duty (a 12-hour stint in the ready room waiting for an alert from the field). The object was (if an alert was called) the aircraft were scrambled and expected to be aloft and heading to their targets in under 5 minutes. During the RIO's pre-flight of my aircraft, I stood there flipping a pancake charge, which is the explosive shell that causes the ejection seat to function and get the officer out of the aircraft should they need to eject, in my hand. The RIO noticed me and asked what it was and I responded, "The pancake charge from the back seat of my aircraft, sir." (Of course, with a very snappy salute) The RIO meticulously inspected every inch of that aircraft until he finally found a minute hydraulic fluid leak and subsequently grounded my aircraft, declaring it unfit to fly. Within the hour there was an alert, Marines were in a bind in Dogpatch (a small village near Marble Mountain) and needed air support. The 3 remaining aircraft took off and when the CO asked about his aircraft he was informed that it was grounded by his RIO as not ready for flight. The shit really hit the fan then, after checking the aircraft himself the CO asked the RIO what he found wrong that caused him to ground the aircraft. After a few minutes the RIO explained about the pancake charge I had been flipping and the CO asked if what his illustrious RIO said about it being from the back seat of his aircraft was true. My response was, "Yes sir, we replace them every 30 days to ensure that the seat is fully operational in case of emergency. I told the RIO the truth he just didn't ask me if there was a pancake charge in his ejection seat. I would have told him the same thing I just told you but he just busied himself with looking for any small thing to ground my aircraft. Sir, my aircraft has a stellar combat record as you can see by the tally of bombs painted on her side. I am proud of my aircraft and keep it fully prepared for combat." Needless to say, the CO did not show great pleasure at cooling his heels while 3 other aircraft were out on a mission. The RIO was duly reprimanded by the CO and my buddies threw me a great party at the Enlisted Man's club. I guess I should have been more forthright with the RIO but "The Devil Made Me Do It" comes to mind. I must admit that the RIO seemed to come off of his high horse after that and did not go out of his way to make our lives miserable any more. Until of course the next time!!!

In order to use my Aviation School knowledge, I was given an assignment to assist in putting up some buildings near our tent camp area. I was one of the lucky guys given the task of "high iron" work. In other words, I was putting up the skeleton of the building using I-beams and pop-rivet equipment to hold them together. Definitely what I was trained to do in Millington (NOT). One day while riding high on an I-beam waiting for the next beam to be raised up to me I noticed I had a great view over the fence into the POW compound not far away. What I saw was very disturbing. The guard (a 6 foot plus soldier) had a cudgel he had made from a large piece of tent pole. He had carved a handle to fit his hand and used a leather strap to loop around his wrist for a better grip. This "tool" was his weapon of choice to extract information from prisoners. I watched him smack a pregnant woman in her stomach with it to convince her male friend to answer some question he was asking. Another disgusting sight was the guards digging a shallow hole in the sand and pushing a prisoner's head into it, covering his head with sand and parading several other prisoners in a circle over his head. The guard would then pull the man up ask him questions and if he didn't get the answer he wanted he repeated the cycle until the prisoner spilled his guts of everything he knew.

The American military weren't the only people who used rather harsh techniques to extract information from prisoners. I can recollect an earlier time working on the flight line noticing a Vietnamese military helicopter being loaded with several VC prisoners and flying to the end of the tarmac. As I watched the aircraft hover about 200 feet above the ground I saw a person falling out waving his arms and legs until he hit the ground and was splattered on the tarmac. This scenario was repeated a couple more times about 3 – 4 minutes apart. The last prisoner was thrown out about 45 minutes later. I was to learn that the Vietnamese Army did this to interrogate high-profile prisoners. They would bring up several people that they knew had little knowledge and one that they figured know a lot of useful information. After asking the useless prisoners a few questions they would kick them out one at a time until they got to the knowledgeable one. After watching the others thrown to the ground the last prisoner would spill his guts of all he knew hoping to be released. The release he got was a kick in the ass and out the door since he was now useless and why feed someone you don't need. The bodies were picked up by a front loader and thrown into a shallow ditch and covered with dirt. This second tour was turning out to be an educational experience that I didn't wish to have in my life. I was ready to go home and leave this craziness behind.

Among the other glorious duties, I enjoyed while with the Black Knights was a two-week stint on mess duty. One of the worse tasks while on mess duty was storing the green body bags of fallen comrades in the reefer to keep them cold until being loaded on KC-130s for shipment home for burial. While preparing a large slab of bacon for breakfast (slicing it into thin pieces for frying) a mortar round landed near the mess tent with a

loud explosion causing my hand to slip and the carving knife I was using almost severed my right index finger off. I went to the corpsman holding my hand above my head to reduce bleeding. The corpsman asked if it hurt and I said I didn't feel a thing he told me I was in shock because the white in the middle of my wound was my bone. I had cut my finger completely down to the bone. He stitched my finger without pain killers since I felt nothing at the wound and put me on light duty because I was right-handed and the cut was on my right hand. He then started to fill out paperwork for a Purple Heart and I refused to sign the forms. I was told since the injury was the result of being under fire I qualified for the medal. I told him that cutting my own finger doesn't deserve the Purple Heart and that honor goes to the grunts out in the thick of it. He told me I was nuts but that is just the way I f
eel about medals such as the Purple Heart.
In March of 1966 I went into Da Nang for my final liberty pass. While walking into the local restaurant district that I frequented an old Vietnamese woman came up to me and said, "Hey GI, soldier need help down here." She was obviously upset so I followed her down an alley to a hooch near my favorite restaurant. In the back room I found a naked airman (his uniform was tossed in the corner of the room) with his hands and feet tied to the four legs of the bed he was on. He had been castrated and his penis was shoved into his mouth and a gag tied around it to hold it in place. After heaving my guts out in the alley, I found an Air Policeman nearby and sent him into the alley to call a medic. I ran back to base and never asked for liberty again. Some sights stay with you forever; this was one of them. I didn't talk about this event until my youngest son took me out for Father's Day when he was twenty-one and asked me if I ever had seen anything in Vietnam that I found too horrible to talk about. He stopped me about halfway through my relating these events.

March 13, 1996, I finally got to see one of the USO shows at Da Nang. Johnny Rivers and Ann Margaret were going to perform so I got there as early as possible to get the best view. I found a place at the middle of the stage six rows back so my view was fantastic. When Ann Margret walked on stage I immediately fell in love. I soon realized why we were there in Vietnam. Even if we disagreed with the war itself and the reasons behind it we were proud members of the United States Marine Corps and served our country wherever they sent us without questioning when or why. Seeing such a beautiful woman perform in the stinking heat of Vietnam and giving it her all made me proud to be an American. I would love to have been able to get close enough to tell her how much I appreciated her performing for us at considerable risk. I mean at least we marines had our weapons with us at all times if needed. The USO performers basically stood on stage being perfect targets for any snipers that could take aim at them. Of course, the area was scouted out before they arrived and the perimeter secured but in a combat zone anything is possible. That show gave me strength to continue while awaiting my orders to return home.

I remember leaving Da Nang, Vietnam March 25, 1966. I was scheduled to leave in two weeks when a runner came to our squadron area and said there were two seats available on a flight the next morning and would I like to leave then. My response to the question was swift. I quickly packed up my duffel bag and went to the departure area to wait for my flight. That evening we, the ready to leave, tired Marines, watched the movie "Shenandoah." Just picture a hillside of battle hardened Marines watching the final scene where the young boy on crutches walks into church and is seen by his father whose face lights up with joy. As I looked around me I couldn't find a dry eye on the hillside. We knew we were going home, and the movie allowed us to release the inner feelings we all felt about getting out of war and going home. Even Marines can cry with joy. After a 24-hour delay (typical military hurry up and wait) our flight left for Okinawa. We landed and within a day I was on a civilian 707 headed to Hawaii, then California. Fortunately for me the only stand-by seat available was in First Class. The stewardesses on the flight were not only gorgeous but very attentive to my needs. Breakfast consisted on half an avocado with slices of lemon and lime to squeeze onto it plus a glass of Champagne. I asked the stewardess what that wonderful smell was that I detected from the lower-class section. She informed me that they were getting scrambled eggs and bacon. I asked if they had one that I could have. She returned with five trays for me which I ate heartily. Free booze and beautiful women what a way to travel home. After landing in Los Angeles, I picked up my tickets for Washington, DC via Chicago. Upon arriving in Chicago, I had a 12 hour wait for my next flight so I called my aunt and visited with them until my flight was ready to depart. They asked if I wanted to call mom & dad but I said no since they thought I was still in Vietnam. My flight to DC landed early in the morning so I took a taxi to Bethesda walked up to our house and knocked on the door. Dad opened the door and was surprised to see me. I went into the dining room and sat down at the table. When mom came in I asked her, "What time do people eat around here?" She was overcome with surprise and happiness and smothered me in hugs and kisses. I can relate to the surprise homecomings so prominent today. Even though many others didn't appreciate the Vietnam era veterans our families did.

1966 Finally I am assigned to VMFA 251 at MCAS Beaufort, SC. This will be my final duty station before leaving the Marines to start college at the University of Maryland's College of Engineering. While finishing my last year and a half at beautiful Beaufort by the sea I had some wonderful memories made. One evening, while checking out a radar unit, we noticed a maintenance person replacing "dead" fluorescent light tubes and carrying them to the dumpster. It is nice to know that we use small fluorescent tubes to detect leaks in our radar's waveguide by passing the tube around the radar unit the tube will glow because the leaking radiation produces enough energy to turn the tube on. Realizing that the armful of "dead" fluorescent tubes may have the ability to glow if hit with a pulse from our aircraft a friend of mine uses a visual bore sighting tool to tell me where to aim the antennae and then I squeeze the pickle (trigger) and viola the tubes in the maintenance man's arms light up magically. He throws them all into the air as his eyes get as big as saucers and he runs towards the main gate. The gate guard later tells us that the maintenance man's feet barely touched the ground as he ran off-base. We also found out that if you discharge your radar towards a drug store in town you can set off a multitude of flash bulbs which you have to pay for when you get caught. Another time a couple of friends and I went to Savannah, Georgia on a weekend pass and on the trip back to base by bus I met an absolutely gorgeous young blond woman heading for Marine Corps boot camp at Parris Island. I wrote down her name and promised to visit her when she was allowed visitors. When I finally got to visit her, she was in the ninth week of boot camp and I found out what the slogan, "The

Marine Corps Builds Men" meant. There in front of me was not the absolutely gorgeous blond woman but a surly looking Marine Corps recruit that had muscles where women shouldn't have muscles and a hard-ass attitude the belied her femininity. We still had a nice visit and I wished her well in her career and returned to base.

While stationed at Beaufort we went on two training exercises under Temporary Additional Orders (TAD). The first was to MCAS Yuma, Arizona. While there a group of us went into Mexico for some bar hopping. We decided as we headed out on liberty to have some fun. One of my buddies took a hot water bottle, filled it up with Dinty Moore's Beef Stew then tied it around his neck under a turtle neck sweater. We proceeded to stagger into a local bar pretending we were all drunk and hungry. Our friend started acting like he was going to puke, squeezed his stomach making sounds like he was really sick and forced the beef stew out of the hot water bottle up towards his chin. As it gushed over the tables the rest of us grabbed our forks and started chomping down the big chunks of stew. People at tables around us were getting sick watching us and the proprietor threw us out. Word spread fast about our little stunt as we were stopped from entering any other bars in town so it was back to base to laugh our asses off.

Our last TAD was to NAS Roosevelt Roads, Puerto Rico for missile shoots. Our pilots were training for air to air combat before being sent to Vietnam. One beautiful day we were working on checking out the radar on one of our birds when we noticed an Electronic Counter-Measure aircraft taking off. I had my comrade in the cockpit try to lock onto the aircraft but each time their equipment broke our lock on it. I then disabled the hydraulics and manually targeted the radar to paint the departing aircraft. Much to our glee it turned around and returned to base. Almost immediately a couple of staff cars filled with officers pulled up and read us the riot act for causing the flight to return. It was destined for reconnaissance over Cuba. Who knew?

After my final military leave back to our home in Maryland I return with my father's car so I can pack my stuff up in it when I get out. My father, being a retired officer still has an officer's sticker on his car so I have easy access to go on or off base during my final months. On one trip to Parris Island to visit my cousin in boot camp I was appreciating the snappy salutes from the recruits when I overheard one of them comment, "He doesn't look like an officer." I stopped my car, got out and reprimanded the recruit for his comment. One of the drill instructors came by and asked what was going on and I let him know what occurred. The DI proceeded to give the recruit a good lecture on why he salutes a car with an officer's sticker on it no matter whom was driving it since the driver may not be an officer but one of the passengers may be. With less than four months left before getting out my CO lets me know that I am number three on the list to be promoted to Corporal. That Friday I was leaving for my sister's high school graduation. Since the actual promotion ceremony was scheduled for Monday he told me to go ahead and put my corporal strips on my uniform for the graduation ceremony. I rented a set of dress blues with the NCO strip down the trouser legs and corporal stripes and headed home proudly showing my father and family my new rank. I returned to Beaufort and the CO pulled me aside Monday morning to tell me that the base commander thought there were too many men being promoted to corporal so his cut the list by one third. He didn't cut the bottom third but every third name so mine was removed. I was not a very happy camper that I held the NCO rank for only a weekend. Two days before my mustering out day our First Sargent called me into his office and had a little surprise for me. He showed me my corporal E4 warrant dated one week earlier, my Sargent E5 warrant dated the two days before and my Staff Sargent warrant dated that day and a very sizable shipping over bonus check to all be given to me if I only reenlisted that day. He also told me that I would spend the next two years at Westinghouse AWG-10 Radar training reporting to a reserve unit for duty once a month until completing training then I would be promoted to Gunnery Sargent and assigned permanent duty station at NATTC Memphis, Tennessee as an avionics instructor. I thanked him for the offer but since I was to start college at the University of Maryland's College of Engineering in three weeks I had to graciously refuse. I did mention that had the base commander not screwed me a few months earlier I probably would have been a career Marine and the instructor duty would have been fantastic. The next day I am asked where I want to be sent to as I leave, my point of enlistment or my family home. Since I enlisted while living in Japan I chose point of enlistment which meant the Marine Corps gave me mileage to San Francisco and air fare to Tokyo, Japan and train fare to Misawa. I cashed in all my tickets, loaded dad's car and drove north to start my civilian life as a freshman at the University of Maryland, College Park majoring in pledging fraternities and going to parties ending up with Lambda Chi Alpha Fraternity Epsilon-Pi Zeta Chapter on Greek Row. My first days at the university were eye-opening. I was greeted by a gorgeous young lady with long hair down past her waist who spit in my face and called me a Baby Killer since I was a Vietnam Veteran. I did take the time to talk to her over a couple of beers and convince her that we weren't all terrible people just because we went where our country sent us. I got into many heated discussions with other students because of this. Another time a friend of mine approached me from behind and tapped me on the shoulder. I immediately grabbed his arm, flipped him over my shoulder and threw him onto the ground. I then pulled my arm back and was ready to crush his nose into his skull when another friend yelled, "Frank, stop!" Fortunately for both me and my friend that yell made me realize where I was and I let my friend up. I guess combat training and quick reflexes can be dangerous. After that incident my friend would yell my name from a safe distance before approaching me. Another incident happened while attending a University of Maryland football game. As the Terps scored a touchdown at the opposite end of the field, a cannon was fired near where I was sitting. My response was to throw the drink I had in my hand up in the air and dive for cover beneath the bleachers. My friends found me quivering beneath the bleachers and pulled me out. I watched the rest of the game but every time it looked as if the Terps might score, my friends would grab my drink from my hands and tell me to "Watch the cannon." They understood that my reaction was due to my time in Vietnam.

I sometimes wonder what my life would have been like if I had stayed in the Corps rather than exiting when I did. Of course, had I stayed in I wouldn't have had my career at IBM that started at Goddard Space Flight Center and the Apollo missions. At the University of Maryland, I actually majored in Electrical Engineering. My first summer break I worked as a summer hire with Bendix Field Engineering at Goddard Space Flight Center in Greenbelt, Maryland as a Manned Space Flight Network technician. The next February I.B.M. had an opening for a Kingston Engineer in the Operations Control Center and offered the position to me. I worked there for all the Apollo Lunar Missions and the beginning of Skylab before the government started giving their contracts to the lowest bidder. Imagine leaving the planet on equipment built by the lowest bidder. No wonder we lost some astronauts due to system failure. I then worked in R & D for I.B.M. developing network cards for the IBM PC, program support for OS/2 and the development of optical storage media. I also worked in Federal Systems Division on the Surface & Ground Launched Cruise Missile hardware and the Advanced Signal Processing System for Trident submarines. I guess you could say I spent the remainder of my 20 years at I.B.M. on the bleeding edge of technology. I ended my career with I.B.M. in 1988 as the East Coast Center of Competency on Local Area & Wide Area Networks.

USMC MILITARY ADDRESSES

ADDRESS		ZIPCODE	FROM	TO
Camp Smedley D. Butler, MCB Hawaii, Honolulu, Hawaii		96819	Oct 63	Oct 63
PLT # 287, MCRD San Diego, CA		92140	Oct 63	Jan 64
"O" CO 2nd ITR, MCB Camp Pendleton, CA			Jan 64	Feb 64
Unit "D" S-13 MAD, NATTC, NAS Memphis TN		38115	Feb 64	Dec 64
H&MS-15, MAG-15, 3rd MAW, MCAS El Toro, CA		92709	Jan 65	Feb 65
VMFA-542, MAG-15, 3rd MAW, MCAS El Toro, CA		92709	Feb 65	Mar 65
VMFA-542, MAG-11, 1st MAW, FPO San Francisco, CA		96601		
MAG-11	NAS Atsugi, Japan		Mar 65	Jun 65
MAG-11	Da Nang AFB, Vietnam	96602	Jun 65	14 Dec 65
MAG-13	MCAS Iwakuni, Japan	96601	Dec 65	Dec 65
VMFA-314, MAG-13, 1st MAW, FPO San Francisco, CA		96601		
MAG-13	MCAS Iwakuni, Japan		Dec 65	Jan 66
MAG-11	Da Nang AFB, Vietnam	96602	Jan 66	25 Mar 66
H&MS-11, MAG-11, 1st MAW, FPO San Francisco, CA		96602		
MAG-11	Da Nang AFB, Vietnam		26 Mar 66	28 Apr 66
FMFPAC Transient Facility Camp				
	Camp Smedley D. Butler, Okinawa	96673	29 Apr 66	30 Apr 66
VMFA-251, MAG-32, 2nd MAW, MCAS Beaufort, SC		29902	May 66	Sep 67
TAD while at Beaufort				
	MCAS Yuma, AZ	85365	Sep 66	Sep 66
	MCAS Cherry Point, NC	28533	Oct 66	Oct 66
	NAS Roosevelt Roads, Puerto Rico	00742	Nov 66	Dec 66
	MCAS Yuma, AZ	85365	Apr 67	Apr 67

The Corps and Vietnam Remembered

Rank I held in 4 years of service in the United States Marine Corps.

    Private First Class   Lance Corporal   Corporal

Ribbons awarded by the United States
Navy Presidential Unit Citation
(with 2 service stars)

Navy Unit Citation   National Defense   Vietnam Campaign
(with 2 service stars)   (with 2 service stars)

Ribbons awarded by the Republic of Vietnam
Gallantry Cross Unit Citation   Civil Actions First Class   Vietnam Campaign
(with Palm Leaf Device)   (with Palm Leaf Device)   with Device (1960)

National Defense | Vietnam Service (with 2 service stars) | Vietnam Gallantry Cross Unit Citation (with Palm Leaf Device) | Civil Actions First Class (with Palm Leaf Device) | Vietnam Campaign (with Device - 1960) | Cold War Medal

Badges

Rifle Marksmanship Badge

Given to U.S.M.C. Vietnam War veteran Frank J. Costanza by President Barack Obama as he said "Thank you for your service." Potomac Nationals Park, Woodbridge, Virginia on September 21, 2012.

About the author

U.S.M.C. Vietnam veteran Frank James Michael Costanza is an extrovert, a Christian, a Sagittarius, a believer in the Jungian method of dream analysis, a student and teacher of "A Course in Miracles," a student of theology and somewhat of an enigma to those whose lives he touches. He believes in the healing power of prayer and inner work, the strength of Christian morals, Christ's teachings on forgiveness and the tenderness of my feminine side. Aside from *The Corps and Vietnam Remembered* he has written a journal of his dreams, prayers, poetry, writings and self-analysis beginning in 1993.

www.ingramcontent.com/pod-product-compliance
Lightning Source LLC
Chambersburg PA
CBHW042052290426

44110CB00001B/35